Day of the Dead

Julie Murray

CABARRUS COUNTY
Public Library System

Abdo
HOLIDAYS
Kids

abdopublishing.com

Published by Abdo Kids, a division of ABDO, PO Box 398166, Minneapolis, Minnesota 55439.
Copyright © 2018 by Abdo Consulting Group, Inc. International copyrights reserved in all countries.
No part of this book may be reproduced in any form without written permission from the publisher.

Printed in the United States of America, North Mankato, Minnesota.

102017

012018

 THIS BOOK CONTAINS RECYCLED MATERIALS

Photo Credits: Alamy, AP Images, iStock, Shutterstock

Production Contributors: Teddy Borth, Jennie Forsberg, Grace Hansen

Design Contributors: Christina Doffing, Candice Keimig, Dorothy Toth

Publisher's Cataloging in Publication Data

Names: Murray, Julie, author.

Title: Day of the dead / by Julie Murray.

Description: Minneapolis, Minnesota : Abdo Kids, 2018. | Series: Holidays |
        Includes glossary, index and online resource (page 24).

Identifiers: LCCN 2017942859 | ISBN 9781532103919 (lib.bdg.) | ISBN 9781532105036 (ebook) |
ISBN 9781532105593 (Read-to-me ebook)

Subjects: LCSH: Holidays--Juvenile literature. | Day of the Dead--Juvenile literature. |
        Mexico--Juvenile literature. | All Souls Day--Juvenile literature.

Classification: DDC 394.264--dc23

LC record available at https://lccn.loc.gov/2017942859

Table of Contents

Day of the Dead

It is Day of the Dead.

Ian celebrates!

It is on November 1st and 2nd.

It is not a scary time. The dead are **honored**.

People visit the graves.

Luis brings flowers.

Ana makes an altar.

It has skulls.

Luna lights a candle.

She tells stories.

People dress up. There is music. Clara dances.

17

Paula bakes special bread.

It is **pan de muerto**!

Alma loves Day of the Dead!

Signs of Day of the Dead

altars

flowers

pan de muerto

skulls

Glossary

altar
made by the family members of one who has died, and usually decorated with photos, flowers, and more.

honor
to give great respect.

pan de muerto
a Mexican sweet bread that is eaten at the gravesite or altar of the dead.

Index

Abdo Kids
ONLINE
FREE! ONLINE MULTIMEDIA RESOURCES

Visit **abdokids.com** and use this code to access crafts, games, videos, and more!

Abdo Kids Code:
HDK3919